PRAISE FOR *INNER SUNSET*

"This book is full of lyricism, animist and mystical often, about the natural world of ocean, trees, fog, birds, insects, and yet, surprisingly and vividly anchored in the city, the house, through windows, walks and wide open eyes. It rewards reading and rereading, as its full context enriches and widens."

> — Barry Goldensohn lives in northern Vermont. His selected poems, *The Hundred Yard Dash Man* was followed by *Snake in the Spine, Wolf in the Heart.* Now he is at work on his 9th collection of poems.

"With exquisite details and simple, elegant language, Heather Saunders Estes invites us to wander into her garden, follow her through "unseen patches of wildness in the city... where raccoons waddle their bulk... parrots swirl on vectors..." and journey to woods, waters, and memories of her past. She touches us with her quiet passion and deep regard for the beauty and terror of nature.

> — Elinor Gale, Poet, Author of the novel,
> *The Emancipation of Emily Rosenbloom.*

"Gently, in soothing *sotto voce*, Heather introduces us to the hidden realms and private universe in our world of San Francisco. In her debut collection of poems, we meet the denizens of the physical world we share — the well-fed raccoons and acrobatic squirrels, smiling at the artful way they walk their wilderness in the streets and backyards of the city. In "Sea Change," her poetry becomes a triptych of San Francisco: "... from our hill house, we see the glint of white breakers between elderly Monterey pines bent in Pacific winds..." Looking out to the horizon, "On windy days when the fog lifts, the far west horizon ... shows profile waves of cardiac rhythm." In "Ice

D1157981

the frigid tundra comes to life: "Beneath me, under stretches of bare ice… Seals, narwhals, jellyfish, almost invisible in the light." And then, without warning, the ice fantasies explode: "At my feet, a carved ivory bear amid bear-sized rocks and magenta wild flowers."

— Elsa Fernandez, Poet, Author of nature poems, including "Bob, the Headless Chicken"

"As natural historian, writing of contemporary life in San Francisco, Estes appreciates the "seal heads of surfers," and the cedar waxwings in their "speed skater helmets." City-dweller, she also knows the public park and the highway barrier, where someone spray-painted the word "RESIST." Techno-savvy, she admits, "I give my credit card to the waiter/ knowing we have all been hacked." In her neighborhood —"They tore down and trucked away the pieces/ of the little 1950 stucco house"— Estes confronts tumultuous transformations. I admire the wisdom in "What they do now can never be undone," even as the speaker finds comfort in "plover hieroglyphs."

— Robin Becker, Author of *The Black Bear Inside Me*

Inner Sunset

by
Heather Saunders Estes

BLUE LIGHT PRESS ❖ 1ST WORLD PUBLISHING

SAN FRANCISCO ❖ FAIRFIELD ❖ DELHI

Inner Sunset

Copyright ©2019 by Heather Saunders Estes

1st World Library
PO Box 2211
Fairfield, IA 52556
www.1stworldpublishing.com

Blue Light Press
www.bluelightpress.com
bluelightpress@aol.com

Book & Cover & Design
Melanie Gendron
melaniegendron999@gmail.com

Cover Art
"Fog in Laguna Honda" by Douglas Gorney
gorney.studio

Author Photo
C. Rutter

First Edition

Library of Congress Cataloging-in-Publication Data

ISBN 978-1-4218-3630-0

ACKNOWLEDGEMENTS

Sincere appreciation to Diane Frank of Blue Light Press for her inspiration and desire to publish this first book.

Grateful acknowledgement to the following magazines and collections in which some of these poems, occasionally revised, have been published: *These Fragile Lilacs, Pangolin Journal, Burning House Press, Avocet, Bach In The Afternoon, Vistas & Byways*, and *Plum Tree Tavern*.

Thank you to my supportive husband and daughter, both talented writers, as well as my very patient friends. Diane Frank is a gifted mentor and my first poetry teacher. The good humor and comradeship of my writing group continues to be a pleasure. Appreciation to Brian Tierney, Barry Goldensohn, and others whose expertise helps garden my poetry.

For Fred and Laurel

TABLE OF CONTENTS

GARDENING IN THE AVENUES

ON THE EDGE

FALL INTO THE NEXT

WETLANDS

SING-ALONG MESSIAH

I

IF THERE IS A WAY

Through Salt Air

On the long turning stairway
up the hill, an old man
sat on the halfway bench,
the one with the view
of the Pacific Ocean sunset
beginning to turn rose.
Was he crying?

A few tourists around,
anxiety, concern.
Climbing up the worn wooden risers,
I hear pentatonic tones
of a Native American chant,
eerie in the growing dusk.

As I climb higher and closer,
the wavering resolves
into Chinese opera or ballad.
He has been here before,
radio in his hands,
music traveling through salt air.

He is singing along
with the lingering, sliding notes
and clashing gongs.
Not words to my ear,
yet I understand yearning, tears,
fury and defiance.

He gazes toward China, an ocean of memories,
from his perch on the steep hill.
I nod as I pass on the stairs.
He inclines a white head
never stopping his quaver-song.

Head-Lamps, Sex, and Bravura

A long expanse of burnt aluminum sand,
tan cinders with reflected sky —
blue slate, ocean to the horizon,
For surfers, perfect waves today,
glass rollers with knife-edge curls.
The breaking surf runs inland
to ripples of miniature sand dunes
incised by plover hieroglyphs,
erratic camels abandoned in a desert.

The afternoon light is beginning to
contemplate sunset.

Seal heads of surfers bob in the waves,
their wetsuits black and shining.
Frozen sand — the concrete wall,
the constantly eroding
Great Highway.

Hidden beneath and under that edge,
unseen by drivers or walkers,
now touched by the first rays of sunset,
are words, huge and emphatic,
fuchsia, red, black, dayglo
spray-painted strokes:

FUCK. The Night Survives!
RESIST.
Ralph was Here!
Afterimages remain, like sun spots —
hissing cans, head-lamps, sex, and bravura.

The Tiled Fish Outside the Children's Library Disappears

Is it a colossal mackerel? In the library entryway garden
a cement fish sculpture,

more gigantic than a coelacanth,
bigger than a swordfish or ocean tuna.

The fish is bent in a U shape, struggling to wriggle back,
perhaps stranded in a dinghy like the Old Man's.

It will flip back any moment, inverting itself,
but can't, frozen in place, waist impaled

with a pipe sunk in the ground.
The tail like a mermaid's, semaphores in different

stone directions. Its fishy expression is surprised,
half-dollar glass eyes of metallic blackness.

In the breaking sun, mosaic skin
of ceramic tiles flashes turquoise, gold, patterned

with edges of celadon and obsidian silver.
What do the children imagine about this fish?

In the night of their dreams, they set it free,
stroking those glorious scales.

The fish sidewinds down the wet sand
plunging into steel blue waves.

Sea Change

We used to live on wetland estuary,
tidal nature dammed, managed,
banks widened and dredged,
controlled by water gates, anti-algae chemicals.

In San Francisco, from our hill house,
we see the glint of white breakers
between elderly Monterey pines
bent in Pacific winds.

The sparkle is Ocean Beach 30 blocks away,
with its rip tides and ice cold currents.
Bones of the clipper *King Philip* sometimes emerge
to caution wetsuited surfers.

On windy days when the fog lifts,
the far west horizon,
no longer flat-lined in the haze,
shows profile waves of cardiac rhythm.

Tower Hill of the Farallones,
trailing islands of Devil's Teeth,
Isle of St James, Sugarloaf,
Drunk Uncle, Fanny Shoals.

Wild places, uninhabited by humans:
seals, sharks, petrels and gulls.
Loud gusts rattle our house,
the glimpse of restless ocean.

If There Is a Way...

crawl under the fences, dig,
find loose boards, gates with broken locks,
leap the passages between worlds

through backyards and dead end streets,
under bridges, along train tracks,

forgotten trees,
around bushes of wind-blown trash,
leaving prints in mud of ephemeral ponds,

following invisible paths
made by generations
of other surefooted creatures,

to unseen patches
of wildness in the city

where raccoons waddle their bulk,
squirrels trip swaying wire paths
across steep, oak-filled ravines,

parrots swirl on vectors,
and children laugh their way
to one lost plum tree.

Green Angels

The morning is luminous,
thick with mist.
Chartreuse, cherry-headed conures
scrabble-fly blindly
to their urgent wherever
invisible in the fog.

They could dive into balconies,
smash through windows,
tall houses and telephone wires,
or get caught in tree branches —
snared and hanging like spring leaves.

They are not squeaking radar bats,
nor zipping, hovering hummingbirds.
Yet, they are saved, time after time.

Perhaps tiny angels with green wings
perch near the hidden red ear
of each parrot, to steer.

Displaced Oven
Santa Rosa Fire, 2017

Exploded
into a sky of flames,
dropping with a screeching crunch
on the blazing house
of our next-door neighbors.

No one heard the crash.
The unexpected flight
doomed smooth white enamel
with cast iron burners and grill
to premature, rusted scrap.

Roaring swiftly past,
the firestorm consumed the neighborhood —
flattened, charred, and stinking.

Before it raged out of control,
tame blue fire
baked birthday cakes, candles and wish,
roasted Easter ham,
fried eggs, sunny-side up.

Water vapor condensed
on floating ash and fell,
pattering and plinking.
KitchenAid logo face up,
no longer of service.

Tree #143

I.

In the city, even the trees
have unique identifying numbers.
Yesterday, a Monterey pine,
three feet across at its base,
was cut down,
trunk left lying in pieces,
too big for the chipper.
The stump golden in the sunshine,
damp and smelling of turpentine.

II.

They are at it again next week,
cutting down more trees.
Chainsaws whine, harsh like dental drills.
What they do now can never be undone.
I watch a slow motion car crash,
bodies piled.

And yet, when they are done,
on this small hill,
my views of Pacific Ocean breakers,
quartz sand flashes of Outer Sunset,
will be grander,
my vision greater and clearer.

I am cut in half.

II

SUMMONING LIFE

Dignity of Trees

Torn limbs expose the inner flesh.
In the small park where we live,
branches hang by splinters
after night rainstorms.

They grip the sandy hillside,
heads swaying, touching.
Their bark streaked in wet,
invisible ravens sheltering beneath boughs.

Too soon City trucks come to cut
and trim each branch.
The old Monterey pines and cypress fall.
Grubs, then woodpeckers — gone.

Better to let them stand,
cracked boughs clothed in dignity,
limbs decaying
in their own slow time.

Blue Moon Eclipse

Hanging in the sky
between Monterey pines,
a glowing, mottled sphere of cinnabar,
a star-flash fading on its leeward flank,
a rainier cherry,
dregs of rosé in the wine glass,
the first super blue lunar eclipse in 155 years.

Six months ago we journeyed
to Wyoming big sky
in the path of total solar eclipse.
A balanced set of sky jewels —
dangerous black diamond
paired with this ember of ruby.

A silver sliver grows, highlighting craters.
To the east, sky is indigo,
pine branches outlined and featureless.
Balanced between the waxing, eclipsing moon
and the hot sun just under the horizon,
a dawn sparrow sings the aria
that summons life into the world.

Fires Burn in Paradise

The San Francisco morning sky
is dirty dishwater,
texture of floating flour dust,
smell of burning electrical wires.

At our coast, silver mists and fog
flow, ebb, stream.
This matte beige air is thick
unmoving, silent.

Code Red air quality looks like this.
Up north, firefighters and neighbors battle, flee.
I sip my lapsang souchong tea,
now disturbed by its smoky taste.

Tomales Bay

Smooth layers of hills,
rivulets of deep valleys.

Rich, feathery redwoods,
steep ravines, black in shade.

Running toward twilight,
water's tarnished silver lines.

Liquid notes of a hermit thrush
sing vespers in now blue dusk.

We will sleep in full dark,
awaken to dawn blackbirds.

Eucalyptus

Flat leaves flash like schooling fish,
swirling shoals in the sun breeze.

Dunes ripple
under the freshwater creek
returning to the sea
beneath mackerel clouds.

Sharp-taloned ospreys
glide above Lake Merced,
spying invisible fish.

It Took Over an Hour

Blue-black bands lighten
the darkest night sky.
House quiet, family asleep.

Now the dusky, sable clouds
glow faintly like banked embers.
Striations of lavender and slate-blue,
then orange and apricot.

The dangerous bright eye is still hidden
beneath the edge of the world.
So slow. Even beauty wears.

Sacramento River

Two tiny rock islands
close to the long fishing pier,
their spring grasses
barely cover undulating sandstone.

A seagull balances
on a rusting pole.
Two Canada geese honk
like Bay tankers.

A winding train lets out a wolf howl
echoing off the hills.

A weathered man
caresses blues from his guitar.
His strings match pitch and timbre
of the train's call.

California Condors

Coal-black pteranodons kite and wheel
on thermals over searing valleys,
cursive waves.
On land, their bodies hump and waddle,
ungainly and beautiful-ugly
with elephant seal faces.

Millions of dollars and human hours
to lift the broad wings
out of extinction and loose them
into the ecstasy of rising thermals.

We try to honor freedom and life.
Condors, health care, justice.
The chasms of need are abysmal dark.

Still, we rejoice in healing
found in sun-glint
off outstretched ebony condor arms,
as new life arises from eating
now untainted dead.

Diablo Winds

The sky's bruised flesh
apricot with a haze of green.

Smoky, harsh air
a cataract over the hills.

Bristlecone and bishop pines
inseminate
the ash-covered ground.

III

SONNET PIE

Ode to My 65th Birthday

A Macintosh apple tree, still some fruit
toward end of season.
Leaves starting to turn red and yellow
readying for winter.
Limbs gnarled, bark rough.
Some in my orchard
already gone to sweet-smelling fires.
The surrounding forest moving in,
bushes, vines, grass long and drying.

A storm comes, but I stand strong,
long roots deep.
Even if I could,
I will not pull them from the soil,
leave the grove, roam the earth.
I listen for stories from the ravens,
whispers from the breezes,
trading ballads, offering shelter.

Faith: January, 2017

The pull-down rusted door
creaks in the wet.
Hand-scrawled sign for one pick-up a day.
Even the inside flap has gang tags.

Does the rain ever get in?
I slide my letter to my beloved daughter
over the small transom.
The post office box clangs shut.

Winding streets narrow down to one lane.
Our cars pass within inches of each other.
I give my credit card to the waiter
knowing we have all been hacked.

Packages collect in doorways.
The locks to our house easily picked.
Yet, we sleep deeply and warm in quiet darkness.
Protected, we think,
but it is faith.

Things occasionally go missing.
A dent appeared by magic on my car bumper.
Alarms beep far away.
I know others are far more unsafe than I.

Still, I smile at strangers in the park,
especially if they have a dog.
I answer my doorbell.
I believe, despite the election,
nuclear war is not imminent.

Recursive

My daughter moved back
into her old bedroom,
jacket on the floor, Ultimate frisbee cleats
drying in the hall,
tofu and miso in the refrigerator,
techno-swing in the air.

My tentative vision of a tiny house
with ordered, scriptural simplicity
of one silver spoon,
smooth expanse of honey-colored table,
the perfect orchid,
meditative, focused, quiet,
to hear myself think and feel —
exploded by one phone call.

My barely accomplished success
creating new retirement rhythms —
tossed, like my unbound hair in a windstorm.

Rising like Cumulous Clouds

Klondike and Sutter's Mill gold miners
snuggled in bed with their sourdough starters,
lusting for morning pancakes, evening biscuits.
New Sourdough Jacks and Jills
search for knowledge and fortunes
in San Francisco's foggy, serpentine hills,
growing start-ups with sugar
from venture capitalists,
all dining on crusty sour batard.

Our sourdough starter first grew in Chicago
fed by my daughter's close friend,
moved to New York,
shared a Boston dorm,
flew west to San Francisco
in a dirty green backpack,
wrapped safely in a pair of socks.

In a drip-encrusted
cherry preserves jar, it thrives —
sometimes forgotten,
frozen in the back of the 'fridge,
underfed, overfed until it fizzes,
stirred back into soft slurry.
Effervescence of desire
with a smell of fresh bread,
a touch of over-the-top ripeness,
growing like love and curiosity.

Red Velvet Cupcakes

with almond cream cheese icing,
still tenderly breathing from the oven.

Crunch of the sugared cake crust
in the midst of sweet softness.
Red from the cochineal bugs,
unabashedly and gloriously fake
like stripes of fuchsia in a millennial's hair.

A classy surprise, pleased
by its own display.

Cedar Waxwings

The sustained medley of quiet bells.
Twelve cedar waxwings perch —
sixteenth notes
on a telephone line.

Their speed skater helmets,
flared black domino masks,
all point the same way.
They flash crimson tips
of eponymous wax wings.

All males, with sophisticated
yellow and charcoal-gray suits,
having drinks at the bar
or lined up at a rugby game,
laughing before they get down
to finding mates this spring.

Frontier

Outside in bare feet
a last-minute bag of kitchen compost
for the green can on the curb.

Black shadows still huddle
about the base of trees.
Tarnished silver sky
holds a line of rose gold.

What is a lone dog doing out?
The dark outline pauses,
motionless in the middle of the street
its head turned, watching me.

We stand, a pair playing statues.
Three or four blocks away,
the elephant trumpet and rumble of a garbage truck.

Damp ocean breeze
lifts hair and fur,
the only movement.
Seconds pass.
I break our gaze first, start up the driveway,
back to morning tasks.

Over my shoulder, the coyote resumes
a slow trot down the empty city street.

Shaker Lemon Pie

Maceration: to squish
the sun-yellow slices of lemons
with sugar, salt and time
until new flavors are released
by biochemistry of plasmodesmata.

That's me, steeped and churned,
submerged in words,
poems, dreams and memories.

May mine — spooned out,
baked in sonnet pie,
flash frozen into tart fiction,
surprise you with a smile.

IV
GARDENING IN THE AVENUES

Sacrifice

Headlamp leads me
down steep cliffs of garden stairs
where the freshest fog-grown kale
awaits my knife.

Crimson veins and glinting chard
reflect the topaz moons
of raccoon eyes.

I wrested fertility from sand dunes
and now I will eat alive
the sacrificial iron-filled leaves
with ginger and apple
sliced for the sharp blender.

From a crystal glass
I sip the emerald blood.

Gardening in the Avenues

Brittle parchment
curls the edges of my Japanese maple,
a transplant from humid summers
where gutters overflow with rain and golden koi.

I too was bred in a wet land,
walking barefoot through rain torrents,
hibernating in white-gray winters.

In sandy San Francisco,
summer is marble and steel skies.
Fog swirls like tides
through our capillaries.

I endure the thirsty drought months,
wait for the first winter soaking
rainstorm with evening lightning.

In fresh-washed raised beds,
now I plant onions and kale,
daffodils and star-gazer lilies.

Lotus

A dried bundle of seeming death
in the dark and silence —
my winter hyacinth.

First roots grow slowly.
Then her densely folded, tender tip
emerges out the bulb.
Tiny leaves are blanched naked,
cold white grubs.

From the downstairs cold closet I carry
the clear glass full of white ghost tendrils.
My table overlooks a little valley
with its flash of the bay,
morning light blinding through large windows.

Sunlight touches the leaves,
within hours, a faint chlorophyll blush.
The first blue-purple bud
opens like sunrise.

Her scent distracts my work
with its subliminal song.
Firm stalk, lavender bloom.

Urgent, pure focus
calls to the bees and butterflies.
Perfume visions fill the room at twilight.

In the Lee

It rained in great sheets, blown sideways.
Now the sun is out, sky bright clear,
heaped cumulous clouds.
I sit in the sun at my garden table.
The breeze barely ruffles my hair,
sweeps my cheek softly.

Yet twenty feet away, gusts rattle the branches,
wind loud in the neighboring grove
of pines and firs. Electrical wires hum.
The utility poles creak and squeak.

When the wind comes from that direction,
my garden cove, close to the house
is protected. The lemon tree vigorous
with its back against the fence,
in the sun, in the lee.

I have been protected from strong winds
throughout my life.
Loving, reasonably functional parents,
sincere and honorable husband.
Great job, money for health care, and comfort.

Where I stand,
the winds of war and despair,
poverty and fear, sweep past me.
I grow my bright lemons
for a touch of tartness.
Try to remember how lucky I am.

Casting a Spell

In the little valley below,
on blustery afternoons,
a mom and her preschool daughter
blow bubbles.
They lift the wand
to the ocean breeze.
The soap bubbles rise quickly,
higher than the tallest tree.
Like a kaleidoscope of butterflies
or bloom of jellyfish,
they interweave and drift.
Caught by a ray of sunshine,
swirling colors briefly glow
like the shine in the little girl's hair
and her squeal of delight.

Resurrection Tree

Lovebird-green shining leaves,
changing carbon dioxide into oxygen,
with promise of astringent truth.
Generations of egg-yoke suns,
heavy on branches, carry clusters
of adolescent green lemons.
Pure white petals
fragrant with the future —
and thorns.

Stars

The kale went to flower
and then seed.

In the midday warmth,
pale green cabbage butterflies
swirl and ride on yellow rockets
exploding out of plant tops,
sparks from wands,
slow motion fireworks.

House finches and titmice
hunt for stars
that cascade to earth
beneath the bountiful sky.

Relentless

A pine-beetled tree, rust and vermillion
in anticipation of the blaze to come,
stands drooping and dying in the public park,
embarrassing to witness, naked in its death.

Beetle larvae and woodpeckers
fat and content.
Crows and ravens eagerly devour
bugs and baby birds.
Red-shouldered hawks
pleased by the upstream feast.

Feast and famine, good-and-plenty.
Finger bones gnawed by worms.
Tatters of skin and clothes.
Buildings in radiation zones,
rust-belt cities, decaying warehouses,
and abandoned farms
decompose.

Recompose as vegetation reclaims,
and yes, the gangs move in,
all living things in the interstices.
Revival, reincarnation,
yeast gives off carbon-dioxide,
bread rises, cheese ripens, beer leaps on ahead.

Here is another poem about death and life,
no indecision,
just the restive in-between.

V

ON THE EDGE

On the Edge

Wind rattles and shakes the house all night.
Monterey pine branches roll
in the incoming gusts
like seaweed under breaking waves.

We live on a hill, three miles from the ocean
where surf rolls in and sun flashes off water.
At the line between our continent
and unfathomable expanse of the Pacific.

Tonight, the air rushes
to fill in a gap in the world,
to satisfy some yearning
like lovers running into each other's arms.

The patio umbrella falls with a crash.
Memories of storms in trees alarm me.
I cling to my husband
as our third floor bedroom sways in midnight gusts.

This is not the ceaseless drone of prairie wind.
It is hungry, whipping fires to catastrophes,
blowing shingles off roofs,
pushing its way through coats and window frames,
demanding, penetrating, urgent.

Garage Door

I discover the door gaping, breathing in
fumes of cold night air over the long hours
since last evening.
The car and cement floor frigid,
damp with dawn tears.

Did midnight raccoons waddle through
snuffling and fingering
our stored books, tools, and bric-a-brac?
Did rats sneak inside,
seeking the warmth of the swaddled water heater?
Maybe they stayed, set up house,
trashing our treasures.

Will I let nighttime thieves
discover the door into the house,
strangle me in my bed,
bludgeon my sleeping husband?
No way to call for help.

Up and down our street
of houses with common walls,
it looks embarrassing,
a woman with no underwear, unconcerned,
her legs casually open.

Decay

In my dreams, houses with leaks,
sagging timbers, soft spots, rickety bones.
My body is my abode
until I return to soil, fire, or ocean.

Time seems to be chewing me,
an old broad, broad in the beam, joists,
glazing going, skin cracked
and cartilage gnawed around joints —
two metal hips, pieces cut out, replaced,
treated with anti-biologicals,
softening all around.

Apparently, now I have house cancer.
My sea-green stucco and wood,
mortgaged home infested with bugs, or mold.
On a San Francisco hill with a bird's view
of trees I love, I am ill
with prematurely decomposing
75-year-old boards and studs.
Not quite my same age,
yet too close to dismiss the vision.

They Are Building a House Right Below Ours

They tore down and trucked away the pieces
of the little 1950 stucco house
on the street below ours.
Every day, rows of flat roofs fill with rain,
bald domes of skylights.

Its absence left a gap-toothed hole between neighbors.
Empty lot quiet for almost a year, yard flowers blooming
for nobody. Two weeks ago, machinery moved in —
jack hammers, back-hoes, bobcats,
dump trucks, and chain saws.

They cut down the trees along our shared
fence-line. The hummingbirds who lived in those trees,
hunting and gathering in my garden,
returned to find their nests and sheltering branches gone.
They perched on the power lines, looking bewildered.

Bereft, I watch and hear the construction,
seeing something new growing, taking root, emerging.
When this house is finished, how will I be different?

Inner Sunset Fog

Fog in San Francisco takes
my mind away.
Spiderwebs become white yarn.

Trees disappear, reappear, fade.
Snow out the window,
steam on glasses,
cotton in my ears,

heavy and flowing
like syrup into our little valley,
or white water, screaming around
the rock of our house.

Is it like meditation on a rainy day?
The house cozy, quiet inside.
The sensation of falling asleep comforting.
Is this what it is like to be dead or old?

Paint it Black

I painted our old fire escape black,
brain cell killing glossy black enamel,
reflecting light even in the fog.
The glittering cut face of coal,
darker than onyx,
the vastness of horses' pupils,
wet raven black,
tar on the road, nightmare black.

I live in a city,
the night sky never this black.
Not the black of black deeds,
black lies, black looks,
black-face or Black Panthers.
No budgets in the black,
black death, black eyes,
black-bottomed cupcakes.

This black sucks light into
a devouring black hole.
The letters jumble meaningless.
Clack, lack, pack, tack, hack
and the newest, frack.
This is the oldest — to burn black,
rushing to escape the bright.

Winged Visitation

Peering down the chimney,
its resonant croaks
travel in the chest.

Scrabble claws
skritch and slide,
tock like hail
on the aluminum flue.

Hops decisively
to the roof edge.

Glides to a perfect landing
on the power pole tree,
preens huge feathers —
obsidian, infinite black
in the morning sun blaze.

The Space between Sounds

1.

The hurricane's roar
falls off to a lull of rain,
gentle rustle of palm fronds.

2.

Two boys whisper as they hide
from the police.
Siren screams down
the darkened road.

3.

Quiet, and the soft slide of blankets
and legs. A giggle.
Lips on beard stubble, rhythm, sigh.

4.

The nurse whispers with the technician.
The Doctor will need to discuss
the radiology results with you.
Please wait.

5.

The machine rockets off the launch pad,
a gentle curve, then explosive separation
of first fuel booster.
Quiet in clouds of roar,
the crowd holds its breath.

6.

Crickets and peepers chorus
from the trees. A loud snap,
a deafening
pause.

7.

A spotted pit bull slowly sniffs
the outstretched fingers.
Holds the gaze of the human
for three heart beats.
Thumps its tail.

8.

At apogee the final firework
winks out, all eyes on the spot.
Then cascades into twinkling flashes.
Concussive bang follows.

Swing Shift

The night heron wakes up hungry,
hunched on streetlights, branches,
twilight rooftops, sailboat arms,
almost invisible
except against the yellow fading light.

Loud and alien
reverberating through the still evening,
a song of almost pain —
not lusty raccoons, not human.
All other birds quiet
but soft-winged owls in the nearby park.

Restlessly walking,
I am arrested by the sound.
The hush and rush of ocean surrounds me
in the settling dark.

Web

In the sun breeze
of a door rarely used
a spider web, each line picked out
like shining metal in angled light.
Train tracks in parallel slightly uneven
wide arcs, a life on track.
Circle lines rattle
alongside last year's rails
funneling over web spokes
of trestle bridges,
narrowing the spiral
into the center roundhouse
slowing to where
end-of-the-line
always
waits.

VI

FALL INTO THE NEXT

Cicada Shells on Trunks of Silver Maples

A gentle breeze from the pines
brings summer cicada song
to the screened porch
of our 1900 clapboard homestead.

Living underground for 17 years,
insect mandibles
push aside spring earth,
scritchy legs laboriously heave
stubby bodies up
rough bark of the silver maple
to reaching height
for a 10-year-old girl.

She is lucky and finds
a creature's husk split down the back.
The cicada already
unfolded like a butterfly,
flown away on its green wings.

Bulbous eye covers, claws
and plump ridged abdomen
imprinted in the amber case.
She cradles it in her hand, fragile
as a columbine blossom.

The cicadas are insistent
this hot, summer afternoon,
spluttering and stuttering
with buzz trills like rattlesnakes.
Their hopeful invitations to mates
fill the fertile air.

Upstate New York

Sides of weathered barns.
Brick chimneys with missing teeth.
One stoplight by the square.
Our faces after a walk through mapled streets
on a 98 degree afternoon.

Catsup with mustard and relish
on pork hot dogs grilled over glowing embers.
Clam sauce over linguine, Chianti in the glass.
Tomatoes in the back garden.
Ripe cherries become a fruit crumble.

Chips of stained glass
in the Methodist church windows
of the town museum that was the old library,
previously the Baptist church.
Worn red velvet 150 year-old carved chair,
only one arm to arrange photographer's subjects.

American flag on the bridge cresting the canal.
Flash of a whistling cardinal in a linden tree.
Rusting shovel blades and tractor parts in pastures.
Sumac torches deepen in color.
Red of unripe thimbleberries
mixed with tasty black.

Imagine the strawberry fields, now empty,
where children of town's leaders bent with migrants,
moved into the hot shed to tally boxes.
The migrants stayed picking.

Hand-lettered signs along the road
for fresh brown eggs,
Rhode Island reds in the yard.
A young fox darts across the road.
Cortland and baldwin apples,
maple and oak leaves
all reds, yellow and orange.

We have left behind
a saturated green land of trees and emerald grass.
The startling red of rust, bird, and berry
becoming counterpoint
in the melody of farewell.

Hometown through New Eyes

Always a small town,
now empty, zombie stores.
Ghost houses
on streets lined with memories of elms.

Our town has a lock on the Erie Canal,
the amazing internet of 1825.
Trains, their tracks laid alongside the canal,
became ascendant within two generations.
Another 50 years, semi-trailer trucks roared
on an interstate built 14 miles away.
Upstate New York villages
lost in their dust.

Medicare friends sit around a table
in the musty 1855 brick house,
talk of basketball coaches, librarians,
priests, mothers, a few friends who moved away
and stores closing.

Family trees of buildings,
lineages of cousins, children, whom they married —
one of those Canastoa girls from over in Shortsville,
they bought the old Smith house, you remember?
Some classmates not discussed.
If you can't say something nice.

Green cords of vines
twine up trees,
choking my husband who escaped,
across the continent.

A few of those who left seem to be returning.
Divorced, leaving the cities
to care for aging parents, buy houses
with urban money, their children scattered.

Glorious summers, harsh winters.
Warm communities, for their own,
not so much for strangers who looked different —
outsiders, immigrants, migrants,
in this town built by the Seneca, Scots, Italians, Irish.

New immigrants and migrants still come.
Mennonites with caps and black cars,
younger generations from Pennsylvania seeking rich soil.
Here and there, corpses of agri-business wars revived,
old farmlands blossom with fruit and care.

Morning Train to Buffalo

Turning window fan,
sun shadows flash intervals
on rumpled bedclothes.
Strobing lights
between clattering cars.

Iron artery rumbles.
Train used to stop in this small town.
Now leaves only the whistle
and older people, poorer people,
as it rattles on by.

Meeting Grounds

The 1697 Quaker Meeting House is full.
Benches face north, south,
east and west, their wood from trees
growing to maturity here, 320 years ago.

Friends and strangers look inward, outward.
In the silence of a forest grove,
subliminal cello strings.
Trees flourish in their own lives,
welcome others to share
the presence of community.

An old clock tocks, like a hooded junco.
A young woman rises to speak
as a sigh passes through the room.
A rustle as heads turn to look, listen,
then return to gaze at the sky
of the burying grounds,
milky blue between maples and beeches.

She speaks about the value of sensitivity
at the risk of feeling deeply.
Her few sentences drop into a
pool of serenity, concentric rings
still into smooth water.

In the calm hush,
greenwood whisper of flame-colored leaves,
winter creaking, plumping buds,
acorns, winged seeds.

One hundred and fifty people, a grove,
a circle, a village, breathe in rhythm,
clasp hands in peace.

Fall into the Next

Rushing through airplane terminals, fumbling
tickets, pages, bags,
very late, can't find the pay phone.
Can't remember the number for my father;
digits squirm out mind's grasping fingers.
Late for the gate, where is the right number?

Takeoff toward a strange city,
plane's transparent side open to the horizon.
It tips, a condor on a steep thermal spiral,
spills me out into cool dampness
of soft clouds,
tumbling the sky toward
a tree-circled pond.

Dive off the dock
into cool leaf-tannin-rich water.
Strike out toward submerged pine tree trunk.
Open blurry underwater eyes,
trying to locate its dark outline.

Out past my swimming comfort zone,
reach down with toes for its slimy, solid surface,
water at chin, arms flailing to keep balance.
I settle like a clumsy heron, wings flapping.
The dock is small, far away.
Wavering shafts of amber light
disappear into shadowed depths.
My unseen toes in colder water,
I have found my own balance.

VII

WETLANDS

Earthwater Deep

Pools, clear springs, wild and cold,
upwelling from secret places.
Forget-me-nots and moss,
thick and deep like the fur of a wolf.
Dig in fingers to reach the earth's skin.

Ponds sparkle with sunlight,
speckled shadows in the reeds.
A brook slides between
lily pads, pickerelweed and horsetails.
Pine logs float for turtle piles,
heron roosts.
A fish leaps in the quiet.

Loons and wild geese wheel and flap
to lakewater runways.
A moving sky reflects upside-down,
gray-green on the silver.

I sit on weathered planks
and turtle-bask, toes in lapping water.
At twilight, peepers and crickets sing.
Night rain drums eternity.

Wyoming Spring

Golden crocus bulbs
slow-growing in the cold garage cave,
settle into our sunlit kitchen,
morning after the March Sap Moon.

Within minutes, a striped bud unfurls.
Another, and another.
Saffron yellow goblets
offer gratitude to the unseen sky.

Above, lavender clouds
suddenly open,
filling the fertile valleys between peaks
with heavy snow.

Hexagonal Crystals

Creeping toward the sea,
glass cliffs plunge into waves.
Huge white islands crack and calve,
floating sanctuaries for sea birds, seal, bear,
while silent life continues beneath.

Ice grows, moves, creates,
destroys, and dies.
Slow language of rivers within rivers,
low thunder, rumbling rocks, soft flake,
sun flash in azure depths.

Decades, centuries, millennia passing,
the earth reveals vast valleys,
drumlin hills, sinuous eskers,
and meltwater kettle lakes.

What does ice say
speaking across epochs?
It is impossible to tell. My existence
is so brief, but I hear
language of transformation,
power of unhurried persistence,
passion of pressure,
the lie of perfect stillness.

Ice Wave

Frozen waves engulf me,
still crackling, like slush.
Hold my breath.
Discover an air pocket.
In my arms a strong rope
attached to the mountain in the distance.
Steadily draw myself up and out, free
into cool air. Surface of crystals
crunch as I walk toward the horizon.
Ice-blue meltwater collects in depressions
reflecting the blue sky.

Lemon meringue sun so warm,
I unbutton my coat.
Thin iridescent clouds float.
Beneath me, under stretches of bare ice,
sea creatures swim.
Seals, narwhals, jellyfish,
almost invisible in the light.

Reach a smooth slope of snow.
A sled, like an ocean kayak, waits.
Slide down fast, paddling, exhilarated,
knowing this is where I should be.
Push, landing on a shore of green grass
under lush oaks. Cicadas buzz,
robins and mockingbirds speak to the forest
clustering and clamoring.

At my feet, a carved ivory bear,
amid bear-sized rocks and magenta wild flowers,
settles heavy and warm
into the curve of my hand.

Frozen Waterfall Climbing Routes
in South Central Alaska

Son of Khan, Bottom Feeder,
Genghis — Flame Out.
No Cigar for the Ptarmigan Couloir
or Death Lizard,
but a Mutiny at the Iron Curtain,
Yellow Fever, the BackWash
became The Lunar Landing —
a 3-Ring Circus.

Fate Is A Hunter, Dirty Harry, Mad Dog,
a Fistful of Snargs, and Vice Gripped
by a Tall Man and an Urban PlowBoy.

Sand Castles of a Dog Day
give Tunnel Vision, then SkyView
of the Rainbow Bridge. It's all a Skin Game,
Touch and Go to Organ Pipes
then Walk In The Woods and Pinwheel
on a Blue Ribbon Ripple of Indecision.
FishRack Traverse Blue Funk
to LineUp on the Spruce Pitch,
turn a Baby Face of Death Valley Daze
to RipTide
and Serenity Falls.

Gray Goddess

Rivers of warm water
flow in the cold sea.

An atmospheric river
pours down on the Bay,
hardly sinking into green
and brown-soaked earth.

The rain gullies fast
in black streets.
Wet people run seeking shelter.
We drive in streams
and our blood moves
in crimson waves.

For just a moment,
a rainbow fragment materializes,
arcing opposite
a misty opening of cerulean.

Even In the City and Time

Somewhere in my city,
hidden between tall buildings and stairs,
— a small, clear spring.

Rough rocks, carved ruins, tumble the site.
Old women honor the ways,
offer a silver cup into my hand
to dip into the basin pool.

Outside is faceless steel, brick,
car exhaust and truck gears.
Crowds hurry past, unseeing.

Young, I drank from a garden hose
in summer heat,
cool water spilling over my hands.

Today, the crones smile at me
and nod — waiting, waiting.
Sweet water fills my mouth,
jasmine, sage, thyme.

Three aspen trees, leaves fluttering,
are rooted deep beneath rocks and cement.
My arms become feathers,
lifting me to song.

Wetlands

Apparently, scientists have found
a new organ in the human body —
the interstitium.

Fluid-filled pillows and watercourses
cushion each other,
like Halloween highway barriers.
If you bump them, they squish back,
like waterbeds, bean-bag chairs,
my mother's breasts.

Blood pulses in rivers, arteries and veins.
I knew that.
Now I am a bog with underground streams,
stepping on what appears to be dry turf,
only find a footprint.

VIII
SING-ALONG MESSIAH

Three Ages of Trees

I.

Three sugar maples, lush and wild,
crowded my bedroom window
when I was a child.
They rustled and creaked at night,
turning crimson and gold in fall.

We roasted potatoes in the ashes
of huge, smoking leaf piles.
In the spring, sweet sap ran fast
in the sun, boiled down
in our summer kitchen.

II.

The ancient valley oak crowned the hill,
proud limbs spread,
a shoal for hawks and squirrels,
deep shade for spotted fawn
in the brittle gold of western summer hills.

I hoist my young daughter up
to curving, muscular branches.
Her small, eager arms hug the tree,
fingers wedged in the rough brown crevices
of her "Grandmother Oak Tree."

III.

Toes sink in rich, dark earth
as deep as I am tall.
Humans and scratching quail
thrive about my roots.
The crown of my head rises in bright air.

As I breathe in deeply,
my heart dreams of moons, turning stars
and the fierce core of the earth
even as I inevitably burn in fire,
and my leaves become the acorn soil.

Whispers

Tiny insects, air made visible,
dust motes of down,
spring and sex
on slow swirl in the sunlight.

Without a whisper
light so softy on my hand,
minute glass wings a lazy flutter.

Tiny faces and delicate forms
drawn in finest India ink.
Clouds of air-plankton,
abundant and certain.

The Back of My Hand

Cords of aging tendons,
cables and wires underneath.
The valley between my thumb and forefinger
folds like hills receding into mist.
Soft eskers of veins,
even on knuckles.
Ridges of ropy lava,
pits, spots, old scars.
So many fine crevices and wrinkles.
I pinch the flesh up to a tiny mountain,
revealing skin's layers, folds, escarpments.
Watch it sink back,
into the ground of my being.

Look Up and In

Stars do not hide
behind blue-black hills
or lavender clouds.

The lights beyond the sky
whirl and burn eternally,
illuminating infinity.

Daily caught by mist nets
of earthbound affairs,
our wings flutter till we are spent,
beaks open.

Unlooked for,
the universe reaches out
to untangle us,
take our measure,

release us upward,
to fly where sparks wheel
in ever-expanding gyres.

Sing-Along Messiah

Is the point to bloom?
Send your sweetness out on the air. Open your petals.
Call to the bees. Lean toward the sun balancing on your tiptoes.
Duet with the rain.

Or is the point to fruit and seed?
Curl yourself into a fertile ball.
Wrap your missives to the future in lemon flesh and thorns
or into maple wings, as sparrows fly west
with your seeds in their bellies.

Or is the point to fade and die into fertilizing compost?
Drop crimson leaves. Sustain the next generation of worms
and lichen with decay. Rattle rhythmic seed pods in the wind.

Or is the point to do it all again?
Come back the next season.
Dance with the daughters of last year's bees.
Scatter seeds, wait with tubers, reawaken.
Send sweet sap up your veins.

Or is the point to tango with the universe?
Feel the energy. Give weight.
Sing your part of the Messiah.
Laugh and run as hard as you can.
Fist bump the sun.
Swing in rainforests.
Spin around the earth and moon.
Hallelujah!

On the Way to Resurrection Bay

Wrap myself in silky smooth
sandy-brown gray of afternoon mud flats,
wisps of clouds on steep slopes — my hair.

Aging skin done in mountain greens,
feet sunk deep in fjords,
light mist falling from sitka spruce tips —
my tears.

A Good Day

Death will not come for me, I will go in.
Crickets strumming, twilight rising,
a swift evening breeze.

Fluorescent yellow ball barely visible.
A sprung thwack echoes across graying fields.
Just one more game please?

I powered the ball all day,
volleyed with energy, mindful of the lines.
The heat of the sun
still a memory in my pink cheeks.

My mother waits patiently,
flowered apron tied.
Time to wash up, set the table,
sit down with the family.

So I didn't whine again
for another game.
I knew it was time to come in.

About the Author

Heather Saunders Estes grew up in a small New England town and now lives in the Inner Sunset neighborhood of San Francisco. The blue jays look different but crows are the same. Fog has replaced winter snow. She transitioned to poetry in 2017 from her long-term career as CEO of Planned Parenthood Northern California. Her writing is inspired by experiences as a social worker and activist, as well as early studies in ceramics and elementary art teaching. Poetry is laughter, reflection, appreciation, and a call to action. She lives with her professor-writer husband of 45 years, and their biologist-writer daughter lives nearby. *Inner Sunset* is her debut book of poetry.

To schedule readings and book-signings or invite her to speak at your book club, please contact via one of the following:
Email: heathersaundersestes@gmail.com
Website: www.heathersaundersestes.com

CPSIA information can be obtained
at www.ICGtesting.com
Printed in the USA
FSHW020045110719
59824FS

9 781421 836300